I'm Not Here to Inspire You

I'm Not Here to Inspire You

Essays on disability from a regular guy living with cerebral palsy

Rob J. Quinn

iUniverse LLC
Bloomington

I'm Not Here to Inspire You
Essays on disability from a regular guy living with cerebral palsy

Cover photo by: John Siemiarowski

iUniverse books may be ordered through booksellers or by contacting:

iUniverse LLC
1663 Liberty Drive
Bloomington, IN 47403
www.iuniverse.com
1-800-Authors (1-800-288-4677)

ISBN: 978-1-4759-9956-3 (sc)
ISBN: 978-1-4759-9957-0 (ebk)

Printed in the United States of America

iUniverse rev. date: 07/26/2013

Dedication:

To the guys I went to school with, from "special" school to the "mainstream"

Thank You:

Maxwell King, for giving me a chance when no one else would and the continued support of my writing efforts throughout the years.

John Ziff, for bringing vast editorial talents to the book, implementing numerous improvements with a writer reluctant to change his work.

Introduction

The word *inspire* has probably become a bit bastardized for me. It's certainly not a bad thing to be inspired, find something inspirational, or even to inspire someone else by personal deeds.

Yet, I cringe when I hear the word.

I want to recoil when I hear someone use *inspire*, even if they are using the word in a perfectly reasonable way. The overuse of the word in describing people with disabilities has created somewhat of a Pavlovian reaction for me. I've literally had strangers approach me at the gym, for example, to tell me that I inspire them. I'd like to report that my physique is the cause of such remarks, but I'd be lying.

Their inspiration comes from the fact that I have cerebral palsy.

Over the years, I've seen hundreds if not thousands of news stories or television programs that put people with disabilities in the role of inspirational figure simply because they are living their lives. The only job I ever quit was when I was given the opportunity to cover the disability community in a realistic way—a concept I had proposed—for the local section of the *Philadelphia Inquirer.* Articles intended to be informative to the local disability community were edited into the typical human-interest stories about the disabled that newspapers have been doing forever. Years later I regretted *not* quitting a two-year job with a foundation—whose mission was supposed to be to enhance the lives of people with disabilities—when it became abundantly clear that they defined my role as a writer in terms of being their inspiring poster child.

I was born with my disability, so maybe that explains why I absolutely cannot comprehend the mentality of individuals who don't seem capable of viewing people with physical disabilities as full-fledged human beings. With all of the political correctness in the world it may seem as though people with disabilities have achieved a level of acceptance where basic statements of humanity are completely unnecessary. But once the surface of that acceptance is scratched, they seem as needed as ever.

I am here to seek all of the same things that anyone else in the world wants, including happiness, fulfillment, success, and finding someone to love.

I'm not here to inspire you.

I've often written about my experiences living with a disability with the goal of breaking the mold of the accepted portrayal of people with disabilities being nothing more than sources of inspiration. "Unsilenced" was the title of one of the first pieces I ever had published. The fact that it was published in the literary magazine of my university was of little concern to me at the time. Writing is the one thing besides playing sports that I don't remember ever not wanting to do. To actually see my words in something that was printed, bound, and handed out to people was the highlight of my college career.

A dramatic monologue, "Unsilenced" featured a high school kid who had been sent to a psychologist after having a fight. The character was highly autobiographical. He had cerebral palsy with a severe speech disability, and was rather unapologetic for finally fighting with one of his able-bodied tormentors.

The response to the story is something that I struggled to understand for years. In the weeks after the magazine came out, I received numerous compliments on campus, many coming from students who I didn't even know but had remembered me from a previous class we'd been in together.

Yet, family and close friends had nothing positive to say. The problem seemed to come from the foul language used by the character. An older woman who I felt particularly close to at the time but has since faded from my life actually told me that I knew better than to use such language. A family member said she put the story down after the first paragraph. The entire piece was three pages. Another family member dismissed it as bitterness.

Later, I attempted to write an actual autobiography. No, my ego hadn't gotten the best of me. My intention was to examine episodes from my life in light of the disability issues that I thought those episodes raised. The book was too long, and no doubt far too boring for print. But the reaction from an acquaintance—a former special education teacher of mine—eventually helped me make sense of the response I had received to "Unsilenced."

I happened to speak with the person just after she started reading my work, and she gushed about it. By our next conversation, however, she'd come to hate what I had written. Her only specific comment concerned my less-than-fond recollections of my time in a special education school.

The man who gave me my first job, and became a mentor to me, would later offer some insights about why my family and friends reacted so negatively to my piece. They had a deep desire to make my life "good," he suggested, and may even have felt a responsibility to do so—just as my former teacher apparently felt responsible for seeing that the special ed portion of my life went well.

My writing about it as less than perfect in "Unsilenced" was upsetting to them.

"Unsilenced" was really about being heard. It was about how a speech disability, or more specifically the way people react to someone's speech disability, can almost dehumanize a person. In some ways it was my response to the ignorance that I had dealt with throughout my life.

Reading the monologue for the first time in years to write this introduction, I have to admit I was surprised by the amount of foul language that peppered the piece. Yet, there was a point to it. In fact, the whole purpose of the profanity was to show a character with a disability going against the idea of "knowing better." The foul language used by the character was a response to the absurd image of people with disabilities that still exists in the media today.

My hope is that the following essays find a middle ground between "Unsilenced" and the attempted autobiography. They represent snippets of my experience with a disability, thoughts and observations on a range of disability-related topics, and an attempt to pass along some advice to the younger members of the disability community. Original versions of all but one of the essays were posted on a blog called Rob Q. Ink—Page 2. (Some editorial changes have been made in compiling the blog posts into book form.)

I've selected the essays from my blog, which almost by definition is meant to address the issue of the day if not the issue of the second, because I think they stand up beyond the moment. The previously unpublished essay was actually written for the blog, and I simply decided to keep it for the book. For me, these essays speak to the general experience of someone with a significant physical disability without any mental impairment who is still able to (or trying to) keep up in the everyday world tailored to the able-bodied. Though some of the endeavors I mentioned are now in my rearview mirror, such as the dot-com I tried to turn into a worthwhile business venture, I think the lessons learned from those efforts remain relevant within the goals of the book.

While the essays are not meant to inspire, they are meant to challenge the version of living with a disability projected by many, and talk about disability from the perspective of an everyday guy who happens to have cerebral palsy.

Wednesday, January 28, 2009
No Magic Key to Life with a Disability

I recently received an e-mail from someone with a disability asking me, of all people, "How do you do it?" At first I wasn't sure what was more frightening: the fact that someone thought they should be asking me such a question or the prospect of offering someone advice about their life.

The individual had reached me via a mutual acquaintance. He has apparently spent a number of years in his home; in fact, he indicated that he hadn't left his room since an accident that left him with a disability. The first thing that struck me was his perception of my life.

No doubt he was offered at least a mildly idealized version of my life, or he chose to hear what he wanted to hear. Possibly a bit of both was involved. He was told that I had been in a similar situation to his and been able to "break out."

I've often been given false impressions—or possibly have heard what *I* wanted to hear—of the fabulous lives people with disabilities are living. I'm typically left wondering what the hell's wrong with me.

But without fail, the minute I scratch the surface of these wonderfully fulfilled lives, I realize the portrayals contain either a lot of exaggeration or just plain fantasy. My point is not to discourage anyone, but to point out a potential pitfall. Believing others with disabilities are able to lead such lives without difficulties is what can lead to being discouraged.

I live with a parent. Last week, which was actually pretty busy for me, was highlighted by going out with a buddy to watch the Philadelphia Eagles and having dinner with a 60-year-old married female friend. I wrote one article for work, went to the gym twice, worked out on my Total Gym, read a little, and tinkered with my website. Besides that I did my stretching exercises to try to combat the tightness that comes with cerebral palsy, and I watched a hell of a lot of television.

That's not a complaint. It's just reality. But if such a lifestyle suggests that I've "broken out" of the isolation that living with a disability can bring, something is seriously wrong.

A big part of what motivated me to establish my website, an online shopping outlet called The Stores @ Royal Steele, and my blog was the hope that I might contribute to changing what I see as society's view of people with disabilities, and maybe even our own view of ourselves. I often read the blog of a guy named Mark E. Smith, who seems to sell himself as a wheelchair guru and a commentator on disability issues. His motivational, ultra-positive messages aren't necessarily my style. But I have come to realize I need to respect the different styles of others looking to positively impact the so-called disability community. In fact, I consider myself a fan of Smith, and I think our community needs more people like him. He seems to be somewhat of a public figure who is talking and writing about living with a disability.

However, one post in particular has stayed with me for some time. In that post, Smith essentially suggests disabled individuals need to simply say "so what" to the obstacles they face and go about their lives. This is a man with moderate to severe cerebral palsy who claims to have traveled extensively, moved cross-country on his own, and become fairly successful in his career.

If that's true, great. Wonderful. But even if it is true, he didn't get to that point in his life by simply ignoring his disability and courageously forging ahead. (Hopefully, the sarcasm dripping off the last three words of the previous sentence is obvious.)

It simply doesn't work that way. Yes, disabled individuals must keep going despite door after door metaphorically and literally blocking the way, even more so than able-bodied individuals. But it takes much more than that.

I've tried to build a network of contacts that will lead to opportunities in publishing, advocacy, and marketing. I do everything I can to increase exposure of my website. Whether it's one more address that will take my occasional newsletter meant to keep the site fresh in the minds of potential customers, or a link exchange that might bring a few more people to the website, I am constantly working to increase the viability of the site.

Progress comes in inches, not miles or even yards. For me, it's the commission that covers costs for the month, or figuring out how to make the site searchable in a way that truly enhances the consumer experience without making profit an impossibility. It's continuing to network for sponsorship when none seems likely.

For years I kept asking the same question the e-mailer asked: How do they do it? How do other people with disabilities accomplish big things, and with seeming ease? What I eventually learned was that these stories are generally told by the media looking to offer a "feel good" story. They emphasize triumph over adversity and downplay setbacks. The realities of being stuck at home, unemployment, and so on simply don't sell papers or grab viewers.

The fact is that there is no magical key. Living with a disability is hard. Choosing to live productively with a disability is even harder. I encouraged the e-mailer to start by controlling what he could control based on the little he told me about his physical condition. Get out of the house once a day, weather permitting, and take a walk. Network via e-mail with friends and acquaintances for social stimulation and to try to find employment opportunities. Contact those within the disability community who can help with accessing needed services.

That advice, obviously, doesn't fit every situation, and the e-mailer may have rolled his eyes and wondered why he'd wasted his time contacting me. My search for answers is far from over. But I was asked, so I offered my best answer.

I think people with disabilities who have the capacity to become educated and work within society can, in fact, "do it." But the "it" isn't going to arrive through magic. It will come through our individual efforts working toward goals we can realistically reach with our own abilities.

Thursday, November 3, 2011
Inclusion versus Mainstreaming: My Experience

Inclusion.

That's the word that has apparently replaced "mainstreaming."

A recent conversation with a friend who was very involved in creating the mainstream program that I attended in the late 1980s until I graduated in 1991 gave me a glimpse of how things have changed since I went to school. I've had other looks over the years when I spoke to a class of Special Education majors at Widener University and through conversations with acquaintances working in the profession.

Somewhere along the line *mainstreaming* seems to have become a bad word. Kids with disabilities now go to their home district at all costs, often with an aide accompanying them to classes to provide needed assistance. It's a side effect of parents who want their kids to be perfect even to the point of ignoring a disability. I even heard a story of a kid with Down's syndrome being shoved into an Advanced Placement chemistry class because "the kids are nicer" in the higher levels.

Leaving extreme examples aside, the image of inclusion that comes to mind is sad: a kid who will be isolated more than ever behind the awkwardness of an aide following him or her around all day. Besides that, inclusion doesn't work from an educational standpoint—even if the kid is in the right class.

Or the young adult. I know because I had a few experiences with the basic concept. Certain college professors refused to go along with the university policy of allowing me to take exams in the Office of Disabled Student Services because I used a word processor. This was before everybody had e-mail, let alone wireless everything.

One genius philosophy professor, who barely spoke English and couldn't understand my speech, showed up on exam day toting a piece of cardboard with the multiple-choice answers A, B, C, and D taped to it. I was supposed to point to the correct answer as he stood at my desk with the board. He was so brilliant he didn't even figure out that taping A, B, C, and D to the board once would have sufficed. He did it for each question. (He apparently had a side gig creating ransom notes.)

A science professor got one of her graduate students to fill in my answers for me on a Scantron sheet. This was better, but still incredibly uncomfortable and unnecessary. Worse, I soon realized that if I waited long enough, the guy's pencil slowly drifted toward the right answer. (By the way, not all of my college exams were multiple choice. It just seemed that way in the basic required courses.)

Besides my lack of assertiveness in insisting that the professors follow university procedure, I think these examples illustrate major flaws in the inclusion system. It has to be incredibly awkward and distracting for the student, and, due to the natural inclination of aides to over-assist, automatically puts the student's academic achievements in question.

Of course, my experience as a mainstreamed student from eighth grade through high school was far from perfect. In fact, it was nightmarish at times. Kids giving me the finger just to see me give it back, as if I were a monkey in the zoo. Teachers giving me decent grades that at times I didn't deserve because they really didn't want to deal with what they assumed would have been a blubbering kid or an outraged parent.

I remember failing my first social studies test in the ninth grade. I failed because my study habits were absolutely terrible. I'd always done well enough studying the night before the test. I was actually in an advanced placement social studies class in eighth grade, my first in "regular school," because of scheduling issues, and I did just fine.

Ninth grade social studies—the subject was U.S. history—was the first class I ever had that consisted mainly of taking notes as the teacher lectured. I began studying the night before the first test, and I even talked my mom into keeping me home the next day to study some more. That's because I knew I had screwed up royally. I knew I was going to fail and I was never more right in my life.

It should have been a wake-up call, and it was for a while. I passed a retest that other kids also got, and I was much more prepared for the next test. But instead of the regular test, I was given the B-level test (which was actually what the teacher used for the makeup exam). Though I did fine on the second test, I was totally discouraged and embarrassed, as everyone knew I had gotten the B-level test. The teacher said I was more relaxed with it.

No, I'd prepared better—that time. Once I knew that giving me the easier test was going to be the standard practice for the rest of the year, I slacked off. I dropped to B-level the following year. B-level was where any interest in a particular subject went to die.

That's just one of the many stories I could tell where mainstreaming went very, very wrong. Unfortunately, I can almost guarantee such situations are only made worse by inclusion.

Yet, mainstreaming—at least the version I experienced—made something available to me that inclusion will never provide a student with a disability: other kids with disabilities. The idea was that the kids with physical disabilities who were capable of attending regular school attended one district in the county, elementary through high school.

Believe me, we weren't all the best of friends, as a lot of people tended to assume. For instance, one day I showed up for computer programming class with scratches on my face earned in gym during a fight with another student with a disability. An able-bodied girl in the computer programming class was confused after I explained the scratches to the teacher. "I thought you were all friends," she said. The fact that we were kids who had simply been thrown together because we all had physical disabilities didn't register with my classmate nor plenty of other people.

But when we were together, that's all we were—kids. We most assuredly weren't "the disabled kid," as we were in our mainstream classes. We fought, laughed, shared answers on homework, and did a lot of the other things kids do. We even made fun of each other. We were kids and we were all disabled, so we were allowed. If someone outside of the resource room made fun of us, though, we wanted a piece of their hides—and don't think we didn't get it once or twice.

We also had one another to talk to. We knew we weren't the only ones having kids jump on the backs of our wheelchairs while teachers watched as if it was funny. We talked about the teachers who would let us slide.

And we grumbled together when the poor excuse for an elevator the district had installed broke down.

One other thing happened specifically to the four of us who were mainstreamed into the eighth grade that first year. Another student had been sent to the same school years before the mainstreaming program was started because she lived in the district. It was her right and it didn't hurt that her mother worked in the district. She attended school much the same way kids do under the inclusion concept. A couple months into the school year each of us was asked, individually, by able-bodied students variations of the same question: How come the other student hadn't done more for herself, like we did? From what I learned it seemed that an able-bodied student in each of her classes had been designated to assist her. Once they saw other students with similar disabilities working independently, they questioned why she wasn't more self-reliant.

The differences in our behavior had little to do with physical ability. My level of impairment due to cerebral palsy was essentially on par with that of the other student. But the fact of the matter was that I was always taught that I would go to regular school if and when I proved I was capable of it.

I fully support the idea that every child has the right to attend regular education classes. However, kids with disabilities are being done a disservice by the idea that they should attend without any burden of proving they have the capabilities to attend. The system has the potential to make us lazy, and hurts the people who truly earn their degrees by casting doubt on the accomplishments of all disabled students. It is also a detriment to our community to dismiss the idea of having

Tuesday, September 13, 2011
A Forgotten Resource in "Transitioning"
  for Disabled Students

A while back I was asked by a therapist from the school system that I attended through high school if anyone ever asked for my input on "transitioning." It's one of those words professionals create. In this case, it's easier to say than "figure out what to do with students with disabilities after high school."

It was a very casual conversation so I offered the easy answer, sarcastically wondering why anyone would want input from someone who has actually gone through the transition. My point being that not only haven't I been asked, the concept of using adults with disabilities to help guide kids and teens doesn't seem to exist in the disability community.

Having graduated from high school 20 years ago in June, my transition consisted of going to college. From there, I had to be an adult and handle my own transition—university-speak for "we can't help you." To be fair, they hadn't been helpful while I was in college, so at least they had consistency going for them.

Yet as schools across the country get under way, I believe the question I was asked, or at least a variation of it, needs to be asked a lot more. Why aren't adults with disabilities more involved in schools? The fact is that universities and intermediate units should be utilizing their graduates with disabilities to offer input on what students should be working toward after the school years.

Maybe I could tell a kid why it's important to not only seek a career he or she can do physically, but one that's in demand. Possibly I could explain why they need to start building personal connections that might help them get a job right now, while they are still in an environment that allows for it. I might be able to discuss why extracurricular activities are important for such connections as well as giving them something to focus on besides school. And there's a chance that, as someone whose been through it, I could help a student being teased because he's "the disabled kid."

People who know me might raise an eyebrow and tell me that, as a teen, I never would have listened to a "mentor" with (or without) a disability. They might even suggest that I was given opportunities to do so.

But the fact of the matter is that I now drive a car because I met a guy with cerebral palsy more severe than mine who drove. It wasn't the point of meeting the guy, but it was certainly the lasting effect of it. If he could drive, I knew I could. Prior to that meeting, I never realistically considered pursuing my driver's license.

The meeting was arranged to allow me to talk to a guy with cerebral palsy who had a job. I was supposed to be inspired, I'm guessing.

I wasn't. I was 18 or 19 meeting some guy I had never met before and was probably never going to meet again.

There were several meetings like that in my life. I remember some guy who was paralyzed from the waist down who swam the English Channel or attempted to do so. He gave a speech at my high school, then met with the disabled students. We were supposed to be inspired.

We weren't.

Now, maybe we should have been. I'm not suggesting that we were right. I'm suggesting we were kids. A one-time meeting with someone with a disability might offer some kids true inspiration, but that's a one-in-a-million shot.

So, maybe I wouldn't have listened to a mentor on a one-time visit.

Yet, since that conversation this summer with the therapist, I've wondered if I would have listened had I known an older person with a disability like mine. No, I wasn't going to make a life decision because I met some guy one time. But maybe if a guy like that worked at my school, I would have gotten to know him. Maybe over the years, the chance to know adults with disabilities could have had many benefits for the kids—and the adults.

The conversation I had this summer led me recently to offer to volunteer at an adaptive physical education program for kids with disabilities held at the university I attended. In years past I have turned down offers to volunteer to speak to the same program. I was at a different place in my life, and volunteering was a dirty concept. In many ways, I still think it is. But I wasn't looking to volunteer in the hopes of landing a job. I just wanted to do something to get out of the house, and hopefully the kids would have benefited too.

Instead of being welcomed, I received an e-mail from the person running the program asking if I had clearance A, B, C, and D. There wasn't even a hint of advice, much less an offer to help, in getting the clearances.

Coming from someone who knew I would have a difficult time running all over town getting fingerprinted and so on, it felt like nothing short of a blow off. This was the same person who was anxious to have me speak at the program years ago. Perhaps it was just a bad day or a momentary lapse by the individual, who I think is a solid advocate for people with disabilities. More likely, I would guess that she just wasn't thinking of the potential importance of having a person with a disability volunteer to work with the program. The clearances are important, but the interaction with an adult with a disability (whether me or someone better) might have been beneficial enough to the kids for the individual to put forth some effort to make it happen.

Schools need to find ways to involve adults with disabilities in the activities of kids with disabilities. It's a basic concept being pursued for every other group of students, and one that needs to happen for students with disabilities more than any other. It might take a little extra effort to get the adult with a disability involved. But whether it's helping obtain clearances, arranging transportation, or even creating paid positions, educators should be making it happen.

My offer to volunteer was an opportunity missed—for myself and maybe for the kids, who would have had the opportunity to interact with an adult with a disability on a weekly basis.

I wonder how many other opportunities are being missed.

Thursday, October 1, 2009
Politically Correct Terms Failing People with
   Disabilities

A recent search of the Web for news on "disability" and "cerebral palsy" reminded me of the illusion of respect for people with disabilities created by politically correct language. The headlines, in fact, reminded me of this not by using the PC terms that have become so familiar, but by using condescending terms many don't even recognize as inappropriate. Just the first page of results revealed plenty of examples.

One story opened with the line, "A bookkeeper for an organization that benefits people suffering from cerebral palsy . . ." I don't *suffer* from cerebral palsy, I live with it. If, in fact, I suffer from any aspect of my disability, society's response to my disability tops the list. It's funny (not really) how we're never described as "suffering" unless the story is looking to amp up the rage over the treatment we're receiving or to induce sympathy.

Another story put the sympathy alert right in the headline, "Cerebral palsy sufferer joins Bobath sponsored walk." The story is about a young girl who signed up to participate in a walk as a fund-raiser for a group that supports people with CP. It describes her difficulties with the physical effects the disability can cause, but she is choosing to involve herself in an event meant to help improve the lives of people with disabilities. The description of her as a "sufferer" disrespects her effort.

A different story included the following sentences: "But that is where CP and Deterding part ways. Apart from being in a power chair to get around campus, he does not really let his illness affect him." First of all, cerebral palsy doesn't come and go. Second, the last time I was ill, it had nothing to do with my CP.

According to Dictionary.com, "illness" is defined as "unhealthy condition; poor health; indisposition; sickness." I work out 4-5 days a week, and there are many who live with the disability who are very active in athletics. The limitations CP may cause can lead to poor health, but calling it an illness is a misnomer meant to elicit sympathy.

Here's another heart-warming headline, "Not Your Average Memoir: One Woman Overcomes Cerebral Palsy to Lead a Successful Life." If this headline was accurate, it would be stop-the-presses news. Unfortunately, there is no cure for cerebral palsy. This woman may have written a great book, and hopefully has some terrific insights into life with a disability. But I guarantee she has not overcome cerebral palsy. She has lived her life with cerebral palsy.

So has the boy featured in the article "A Scout is courageous." He is described as one who is "battling cerebral palsy" and "didn't take an easy route to the honor of Eagle Scout." And despite this headline's claim, "Cerebral palsy can't slow down a local entrepreneur," I'd bet my last dollar that the disability most certainly has slowed the person down.

Now, most people have likely stopped reading or have concluded that I'm just some bitter disabled guy. (Oops, hopefully they referred to me as a bitter person with a disability, because that's the proper way to refer to us in the PC world.) Of course, these are the same individuals who think people with disabilities are here to inspire the able-bodied and go away quietly when that chore is done.

If anyone thinks I'm criticizing the people in these stories, they're simply not paying attention. The criticism is with the media outlets that, whether intentionally or not, are actually degrading these people to make their stories more palatable to their mostly able-bodied readers.

No one buys a paper or clicks on a news story to read about the realities of life with a disability. Words like "overcome" and "part ways" and "battling" play into the Sunday Night Movie mentality of years ago, suggesting that the disability is ultimately going to disappear or that there's something heroic about living your life with a disability.

Here's the problem with that besides what should be the obvious moral issue: No one listens to the *real* issues in the disability community. Why should they? According to the media, if those of us with disabilities just tried hard enough, we would overcome our pesky little disabilities.

Society has been handed the bogus "issue" of calling disabled individuals "people with disabilities" because they can grasp it. The public's 2-second attention span makes it possible for everyone to remember to use "people with disabilities." This use of politically correct terminology is supposed to equate to an enlightened society and an improved existence for people who can't walk, or can't see, or have difficulty speaking.

I'm tempted to use more sarcasm here, but it would fly over the heads of those who actually need to get my point: I am disabled. The word is perfectly accurate to describe how my body functions in some ways, and how society allows me to take part in the able-bodied world. The notion of what I've heard termed "people-first language" changing the way people perceive those of us with disabilities is a pipe dream and the concept itself is actually patronizing. Replacing the word *disabled* with the phrase *people with disabilities* has been a colossal waste of time. It has completely failed in its objective to change the perception of those of us living with disabilities.

I've now worked for three bosses who had PC language down to a tee, yet all were incredibly patronizing and none showed any inclination to elevate my salary to a level commensurate with my education and experience. One was even the mother of a son with CP. She ran one of those faux nonprofits that supposedly helps the disability community but really just keeps a few able-bodied folks employed. She treated me like a poster child for two years, and when I refused to write a report for the organization that provided the endowment that paid for my position, she informed me that she would not patronize me and that my refusal was unacceptable.

The minute someone announces they're not going to patronize another person, it's a safe bet they are already doing just that. In a professional disagreement, my former boss felt compelled to tell me she would not patronize me. (Having done it for two years, maybe she at least had a thought of trying something new.) Yet the mere reference to the idea that she would be patronizing me if she accepted my stance is patronizing. It suggests that a person with a disability couldn't possibly disagree with an able-bodied person and be allowed to "get away with it" unless the disabled person was being patronized. (By the way, I later confirmed with the endowment that I didn't have the right to see the report my boss tried to get me to write. Obviously, it was my boss's responsibility to prepare.)

Personal venting aside, the point is that handing people like my ex-boss a mask of politically correct terms to hide prejudiced behavior only complicates problems for those with disabilities. The argument, as I understand it, is that using the word *people* or *person* in phrases like "person with a disability" stresses that we are people first and we happen to have a disability.

Hello?

I don't know who decided we had given up this assumption that we are part of the human race, but I sure as hell did not. Actually, I know exactly who decided it: the so-called advocates who supposedly work to improve the lives of people with disabilities.

I've known many disabled people—yeah, I said it—throughout my life. Not once, not a single time, have I ever been in a casual conversation with other people with disabilities in which anyone has uttered the phrase "people with disabilities" or given a damn about being called "disabled." Yet, I've had able-bodied people read articles or fiction of mine involving disability issues and take it upon themselves to tell me that using "disabled people" is a problem with my work. The entire "issue" has been created by the able-bodied professionals deciding how to discuss us. Now *that's* insulting! They are the ones who have decreed what is the proper way to refer to someone with a disability.

Referring to us in these politically correct terms was somehow going to change the way able-bodied people perceived us. Oh, how wonderful! Too bad it was a ridiculous notion that has failed miserably.

Politically correct language is clearly not enough. In fact, it's become a hindrance. For evidence, just check out the news focused on the disability community every now and then.

Tuesday, August 24, 2010
Hierarchy of Disability Weakens the Community

One of the first pieces of writing I ever published was a dramatic monologue in the yearly collection of student works that my university put out every spring semester. In the story a teenaged kid with a speech disability is sent to a psychologist after getting into a fight at school with classmates who had teased him about his speech.

A few weeks ago as I was posting videos on PhillyACCESS, an informational blog I produce for the disability community, the monologue came to mind. The series of videos from the American Association of People with Disabilities featured numerous individuals talking about the Americans with Disabilities Act in celebration of the law's 20th anniversary. Having discovered the series a few weeks after it had begun, I was sharing the most current video in the series with PhillyACCESS readers as they were released. After a few posts, I started to realize that not a single person in the videos had a speech impairment, except for a deaf individual whose words were spoken by someone off camera as she signed.

Ultimately, I discovered that one of the early videos did have someone with a somewhat mild speech disability. But just the one.

Not only did the scarcity of speech disabilities in the series bring my dramatic monologue to mind, but it made me wonder about the validity of the idea that a hierarchy of disability exists even within our own community.

There were very few visual indicators of disabilities in any of the videos. One man's wheelchair was visible due to a high back. Again, the two individuals mentioned above had communication disabilities that were evident. The co-founder of the AAPD has artificial hands that were clearly shown. Besides that, one individual was blind, which was noticeable only because she mentioned it, and another guy had glasses that might or might not have been related to a disability other than aging eyes.

I don't mean to pick on the AAPD. I noticed the same phenomenon in a recent public service announcement meant to encourage the hiring of people with disabilities. The woman featured in the PSA, though using a wheelchair (a very old model that likely had come from a prop room), was perfectly able-bodied from the waist up as far as a viewer could tell.

In this age of overbearing political correctness and inclusion at all costs, it's beyond distressing to see that the disability community itself is coming up short in this area. Everyone in the community who was born with a disability, as opposed to those who became disabled, has known for ages that the hierarchy exists. The language and the public images have made it clear for as long as I can remember.

Talk of employment focuses on getting people with disabilities "back into" the workforce. We have the Office of Vocational Rehabilitation. The word *rehabilitate* suggests a need to recover from, instead of live with, a disability. Therapy is often provided in rehabs. Forms for Social Security Disability and the like incessantly assume that a disability has occurred sometime after birth and/or comes with a termination date. More and more, disabled veterans and aging issues are lumped together with disability material. Today, we even have a character in the Fox show *Glee* who fits the accepted public image of disability—essentially able-bodied except for the use of a wheelchair.

The reaction I received to "Unsilenced," the monologue published in the university literary magazine, was quite telling in the end. For the only time in my life people who barely knew me went out of their way to say they liked something I'd written. I had an art history professor tell me (during class) to keep writing because she liked the piece so much.

Yet, the people who knew me best hated the piece. They were unable to separate the character from myself. More to the point, they were unable to get beyond the foul language used by the character early on in the play to see the reason for it because they saw it as coming directly from me.

As I tried to convey all those years ago, there is something intrinsic about being able to understand what someone says. There is an assumption that someone who cannot physically speak clearly is unintelligent. The words are unintelligible, therefore (the assumption goes) so are the thoughts being expressed. Even people who are very close to individuals with speech disabilities, which are often accompanied by other upper-body disabilities, often show signs of paternalism toward the person with the disability. Strangers often react to not being able to understand what someone is saying by pulling away. They are somehow embarrassed, and they want to disconnect as fast as possible. Even when a speech disability is not part of the equation, the spastic or jagged movements from an upper-body disability act as triggers for these type of reactions.

I was on the campus of Widener University a few years back to talk to a class of prospective special education teachers. I was looking for the building in which the class was to be held, and I tried to ask two women dressed in nurses' apparel for assistance. They originally slowed down, obviously willing to help, when I made eye contact. After they heard my voice, however, they picked up their pace and hustled right by me as though I were invisible. One had the nerve to look back at me and shrug as if there was nothing she could do about her completely inappropriate response. Unfortunately, there was nothing I could do about their completely inappropriate career choice.

Would they have stopped for someone who did not have a speech disability? Obviously, I can't prove it, but I'd bet a whole lot of money that they would.

In a very real way, these inappropriate reactions are being fostered by the disability community itself. The fact is that the general public sees an image like the character on *Glee* and accepts it as the image of someone with a disability who can be a functioning member of society. There's simply not enough images of disability in the mainstream media for them to do anything else. It's the image they may actually become comfortable with some day, which leaves out anyone and everyone that doesn't fit the image. If the general public ever actually see someone with disabilities affecting upper-body motor skills, the person is usually appearing on a telethon or an actor is playing a role in a Hallmark Channel movie looking to elicit pity.

Yet, we can't blame Hollywood when our own community produces a series of videos and PSAs that don't do any better.

If we are unwilling or unable to change that accepted image of the person with a disability who is a full-fledged member of society, we are sentencing a large segment of our community to prejudiced treatment that is essentially viewed as "OK."

If we continue to allow a hierarchy to exist that puts the "less physically disabled" individuals at the top with the "more physically disabled" below, we have no disability movement. We are essentially going with Darwin's "survival of the fittest" theory. At the very least we are guilty of the same offences we love to pin on the able-bodied world, and we can stop what would appropriately be seen as the nonsense known as the disability movement.

Or we can truly insist that our community—in its entirety—be unsilenced.

Tuesday, June 16, 2009
Do-it-yourself Therapy

Thirty-five minutes a day. That's how long I stretch my hamstrings. To be completely accurate, I average 35 minutes a day of stretching, often doing double duty once in a given week or performing an extra few minutes per day to make up for a day I missed.

I've been stretching regularly for about five years now. I started off with five minutes a day, Monday through Friday, as my goal. I was only using five-pound dumbbells, resting one just above each knee as I sat against the couch (or whatever) with my legs out in front of me.

I'm now up to 20 pounds resting on each leg, but I honestly don't know if I've made any real progress over the years. Certainly my tolerance has improved, but my legs don't seem to be able to extend any straighter than they could when I first started doing the stretching regularly. The only thing I feel confident saying is that I've stopped any regression from spending most of my waking hours in a seated position with my legs bent at a 90-degree angle.

My guess is that what I really need is someone to push on the legs better than I can do with the weights. What I really need is the therapy that was available to me as a kid up until I was mainstreamed.

At that age, I didn't understand the importance of keeping up with my therapy, and it was never really explained to me well enough. At a very young age I abandoned, and was allowed to abandon, braces that went from my calves to my toes because they dug into my legs and feet when I crawled around to play. Questions, no doubt whiny ones, about why I needed to stretch were answered with overly simplistic suggestions that I wouldn't be able to move when I was older if I didn't.

Well, that didn't register with me as a kid. I was young, could bounce around on my knees with no problem, and using a wheelchair really didn't seem like a big deal. I knew pretty young that walking wasn't the Holy Grail of people with disabilities that it's portrayed to be by the media. The spasticity caused by my cerebral palsy made it clear that I wasn't going to be walking around school or the adult world. It just wouldn't be safe, and, considering the need to carry books at the time or any number of other things in the future, walking may have actually made me less independent in some ways.

Not that I didn't try. I used a walker for several years, and at one point for about six months, maybe more likely six weeks, I used one crutch. I even walked without any assistive device for a short time. The need to go from point A to point B earned me the nickname of Crash Quinn for some. But none of those options ever seemed realistic for moving around in the "real world" that I was always being told I'd have to enter someday.

What I didn't realize was that it would be nice to walk from point A to point B in my home as an adult. Or that entering someone's home or a restaurant using a walker might be a lot easier than always needing a wheelchair. It didn't necessarily have to be the all or nothing proposition that was presented to me, or quite possibly that I made it out to be in my own head.

I didn't realize that, sure, I'd be able to move around without stretching and braces when I was in my 30s. But it would be a hell of a lot easier now if I had continued the therapy and the use of braces through the years.

As I've looked to restore these options in my adult life, I've discovered an almost complete lack of services readily available to adults with disabilities who seek to resume the physical therapy they (hopefully) had throughout their childhood. The health craze that hit in the '80s and continues somewhat today, makes the hardest part about finding a trainer sorting through the many options likely found within a 3-mile radius of a person's home. Yet finding options for physical therapy to simply maintain flexibility or address similar issues that are caused by a disability like cerebral palsy seems to be impossible.

I went to one doctor in the last several years who wanted to inject my legs with Botox every three or four months to relax my hamstrings. I actually tried it once, and the best way I can describe it is that it felt like having fire injected into my legs. In high school I briefly attended therapy at one of the rehab centers of the fitness guru and entrepreneur Pat Croce, though my main interest in going at the time was weight training. It was great, except for the fact that my insurance treated each session like a doctor's visit, for which I needed a prescription that may or may not be renewed by the proper specialist every few months. My aversion to doctors and impatience with "the system" cut the experience short. I've even heard stories of trainers literally backing away from people inquiring about having them help with their therapeutic exercises.

This isn't meant to be about blame, or even a cautionary tale. Instead, my intent is to simply share my experience, encourage others to do the same, and hopefully learn a thing or two from thinking about how

I've gotten to this point in a serious enough manner to write about it. If a reader learns something or simply has an idea sparked by this essay for their own therapy, even better.

The best solution I've found for maintenance therapy is the do-it-yourself approach. So, today I'll continue with my weekly routine of biking (either 35 minutes on the stationary or a few miles on the new adaptive bike I just bought), 150 crunches, and 35 minutes of stretching. Usually Tuesdays are my Total Gym days instead of biking, but two days on the adaptive bike over the weekend made switching things up a must.

From time to time I'll also continue to wonder if I could have been a little better off had I been taught a little more about what I needed to be doing when I was a kid—and had I been a little more mature and a little less stubborn about doing it. But while I might be able to walk into a restaurant or get around my own home with some type of walker, I doubt my mobility would be much better than it is right now.

Hopefully, I'll also continue to at least maintain if not improve my mobility. By writing about my experience so far, maybe I'll help a teenager or two not have to wonder about what they should have done as kids when they are looking back 20 years from now.

Tuesday, January 4, 2011
The Worst Advice I Ever Received

Don't lift weights.

That's right, *don't* lift weights.

Years ago, when I sought advice on how to enhance my weight-lifting routine, I was advised by more than one doctor that I shouldn't be lifting weights at all. Luckily, I chose not to listen.

I'm not a doctor, nor do I play one on TV. This essay is not meant to encourage anyone to dismiss their doctor's advice. But as the gyms of America fill up with people energized to keep their New Year's resolution to get in shape, I wonder how many people with disabilities have been encouraged to do the same thing.

I was in my late teens when I first heard the advice not to pursue weight training. I heard it again in my 20s, and more recently—and in a very specific manner—in my 30s.

The theory has always been that because I have cerebral palsy, I shouldn't be doing anything to tighten my muscles. I already battle tightness in my hamstrings that keeps my legs from extending fully. I was also told weight training would increase my spasticity.

Yet, even the first time I heard this advice, I had already been lifting weights for several years. I began in earnest the summer before I started high school, with thoughts of trying to be part of the wrestling team. A friend of mine had previously been a member of the team, and another was going to give it a shot the following year. Both had mild CP compared to mine, and were very muscular—"huge" was the term appropriately used for them—from years of lifting weights.

Wrestling never quite worked out for many reasons, not the least of which was seeing a teammate barf one day and hearing a coach say it would help him make weight. I also recall a T-shirt depicting the evolution of man, with a basketball player at the beginning and a wrestler at the end. My thinking was pretty much the opposite. When I told a classmate to stop pushing me as I used my manual wheelchair during cardiovascular work one day, he responded by saying, "C'mon, Robby, you're not doing anything anyway. Let me coast."

Clearly, I was in the wrong spot. I didn't even weigh enough to wrestle in the lowest weight class anyway. While my wrestling career only lasted a week, I've been lifting weights pretty much ever since.

I've certainly never gotten "huge," but weight training has helped me throughout my life. I graduated high school and college, obtained my driver's license, worked full-time for several years, and lived semi-independently in my own apartment—all the while continuing to work out. Had the weight training caused the effects of my CP to get worse, it would have made all of those accomplishments more difficult, if not impossible, to achieve.

In fact, I believe lifting weights *helped* me in some of those endeavors. I'm not sure that I would have made it through the adaptive driving program without lifting weights. The constant turning during lessons put a strain on my right shoulder as I use a steering knob for one-handed driving. The strength I had built up definitely helped me get through the lessons. These were lessons that I was almost denied twice, the second time when the coordinator of the adaptive driving program went to my mom and told her that, based on the level of my CP, he could disqualify me at the outset if she wished. She didn't. It's not hard to see how a little less strength on my part could have been the final straw for the coordinator to disqualify me even without my mom's blessing.

More recently, I was told not to do exercises to increase the strength in my forearms as it would cause my hands to tighten up. Unfortunately, I actually listened to this advice until the last few months.

Coming down the home stretch of the M.S. Ride in September—a 75-mile journey from Cherry Hill to Ocean City, New Jersey—I was completely worn out and didn't have the strength to shift gears on my adaptive bike. It's a mistake I don't intend to repeat. The "hand grip" has been taken out of the drawer and is getting regular use.

Of course, if I had given up weight training when I was told to, I would never have taken on the challenge of the M.S. Ride in the first place.

I also wouldn't be going to the gym three or four times a week. I wouldn't be getting out of the house on a regular basis now that I'm unemployed—or underemployed, as I do take my own writing efforts seriously—and interacting with at least a few people at the gym. I also probably wouldn't have gotten into the adaptive cycling program that is now a big part of my life and has connected me with the best group of people with disabilities that I've ever been a part of. As a result, my days would be more monotonous with much less human interaction.

The increased spasticity and decrease in flexibility that I was warned about simply never happened. To look at me, no one would ever guess that I've lifted weights for years, but I know I've increased my upper body strength. While range of motion has never been a big issue in my upper body, I have made a concentrated effort to increase the flexibility in my legs over the last seven years. I can't say that the stretching I do for my hamstrings has been particularly effective, and I do avoid leg curls in my workout routine. Yet, my strength and endurance have only increased, especially in the last few years.

If pedaling 75 miles in one day doesn't prove that, nothing will.

At one point I did give up lifting heavy weights. When I joined the gym, I was taught the routine of training one body part a day. It was quite effective; I made my greatest gains ever. But my joints eventually couldn't take the amount of weight I was lifting—heavy for me, though not for most people.

I finally fully accepted that with cerebral palsy and a slender build, "getting huge" wasn't going to happen for me. But I still wanted to work on my strength, so after the joint pain receded I decided to go back to using the Total Gym, which I had used on and off for years. I've been told I sound like a spokesman for the product, which *is* very effective. Plus, I didn't experience any joint pain when I used it.

After the M.S. Ride, however, I felt like I needed more strength. So, after a break of a couple of years, I've returned to lifting weights twice a week with the machines at the gym. I also still ride the exercise bike at least twice a week. I stay away from the dumbbells and the Smith Machine (also called the Squat Rack, from what I've heard), which simulates free weights better than the more popular machines for some exercises like the bench press. I believe the Nautilus/Cybex machines help me do the exercises with better form, and not trying to move benches around or take plates on and off the bars is a big plus. I'm also slowly testing how much weight my joints can bear.

I feel better lifting weights. Stronger. I'm motivated to increase the amount of weight I can lift, though slowly and cautiously. I'm even getting more of the well-documented benefits of weight-bearing exercise.

So, I'm left to wonder just why doctors were so quick to tell me *not* to lift. I remember one doctor essentially dismissing the fact that I had already lifted weights for years with many benefits before seeing him. It simply didn't matter to him. The thinking at the time was that lifting weights might have negative effects for someone with cerebral palsy, and my experience meant nothing.

To be fair, my family doctors (there have been two since I was a kid) never discouraged my workouts, and I currently go to a chiropractor who supports the activity as well. Even back in high school, I met a guy with mild CP who ran a gym and had worked out for years. As he explained, the theory that lifting weights would decrease my flexibility was incorrect, provided I did the exercises with a full range of motion.

Did the doctors simply give me bad advice based on thinking that, at the time, was just beginning to become outdated? I doubt it based on the advice I received about strengthening my forearms. My guess is that the bad advice had far more to do with the perceptions of people with disabilities.

The specialists who told me not to lift weights didn't know me. They simply saw a guy with moderate to severe cerebral palsy, and "read from the textbook." There was no give-and-take. No desire on the part of the doctors to modify the specifics of my workout regimen. There was certainly no thought given to the ancillary benefits of exercise, such as getting out of the house, interacting with others, and so on.

Things have improved since then, but I wonder how many doctors would offer—and do offer—the same textbook advice today. Hopefully, one of these years when I return to the gym after the holidays, there will be another guy or woman with a disability—or two or three—adding to the gym population that always seems to grow around this time of year.

Maybe they'll even be there because of some *good* advice from a doctor.

Thursday, February 9, 2012
From the Heart, About the Heart

Writing about love is kind of like writing about politics for me. I don't know much about it, and I haven't participated in the process very much. I've never had a relationship with a woman, at least not a relationship that was intended to be anything beyond friendship. In fact, I've only had one to three dates depending on how far the definition of the word *date* can be stretched and whether or not the senior prom counts. I'm guessing it does not.

For me—and I have to say "for me" because I know of others for whom this is not true—disability is woman repellent. I'm a fairly average guy in many ways: love sports, have a college degree, worked out regularly most of my life, etc. I just turned 40, and enough people tell me I still look like I'm in my 20s that I assume there's some truth to it. In some ways that might not be a good thing.

I've even been told that the one definite date I had could have become a second had I been interested. Unfortunately, there just wasn't the slightest spark of interest for me. And when I say "unfortunately," I mean it. I wasn't confused, or shy, or anything else. I absolutely wanted to feel some spark with the woman; even the faintest of hopes that I could have been interested in her would have sufficed. I don't say that to be obnoxious. She just wasn't a match for me.

The date came about through an organization whose name incorporates a cutesy play on the word *disabled*—along the lines of the made-up word *handicapable* that was in vogue years ago. My one-year membership with the organization got me exactly one profile of a woman in my area. The idea of a dating service for people with disabilities seemed like a good idea, but, at least with the organization I joined, that idea doesn't seem to be executed all that well. The website encourages members not to limit their search to a local area. This is no doubt a good business move allowing them to claim more "connections." However, an e-mail exchange with a woman who lives far away, and who (like me) probably has difficulty with long-distance travel, isn't a pairing I'd call "able" to date.

At one point I actually considered going on a cruise sponsored by the organization. When I asked too many questions about accommodations, I was told not to worry and just go for it. If others in need of assistance with some of the basics that go along with such a trip can do that, more power to them. It wasn't for me.

There was a time I wondered if I could be interested in dating a woman with a disability. Many may be horrified by such a revelation. Recent interactions, while not leading anywhere, have dispelled those doubts to a large degree. However, if I'm being completely honest, the women I've found appealing are more able than I am in some ways.

Is it self-loathing? I don't think so, but I'm sure there's some line of psychological thought that would put such a label on it. I think some of my feelings may come from the fact that I deal with my own limitations enough, and I don't want to deal with similar physical disabilities in someone else.

I'm far from alone in having questioned whether or not I would want to date another person with a disability. When I was a teenager, the girls with disabilities I knew swooned over every able-bodied son of a teacher who ever showed his face at our school—a school for kids with disabilities. The guys pretty much had the same attitude toward girls. Though there were a few dates among the students, a date with an able-bodied person was seen as somehow better.

I was once told a story of an engaged couple, both of whom had disabilities, in which the woman eventually broke the engagement. She used aids to get through much of her day, while her fiancé preferred to do things independently. She tired of waiting.

At least if I'm an asshole for having felt these doubts, I'm not alone.

The question is obvious. How the hell could I hope to find someone with the patience to deal with my disability when I didn't have the same ability for her?

I don't have an answer to that, except that we're all human and eventually most of us mature.

To be fair, if I include the prom, the two dates I've had were with women who have cerebral palsy much like mine, and I can honestly say that their disabilities were not issues for me. In some ways, I wondered how much at least one of them accepted her own limitations. In neither case, however, was the woman's disability the reason we didn't have a second date.

Of course, a large part of finding love involves sex. It's probably been the most frustrating part of my life. I've heard a little bit about the new film *The Sessions*. The Internet Movie Database summary of the movie reads, "A man in an iron lung who wishes to lose his virginity contacts a professional sex surrogate with the help of his therapist and priest." I'm told there are differences between a surrogate and a prostitute, and I don't mean to quibble over them here. But the attention that the film received brought to mind my own thoughts of hiring a prostitute.

For now, I just don't see much of a point to dealing with the issue of a lack of sex by hiring a prostitute. Believe me, I'm not "saving myself" for true love. I just don't know what has really been accomplished once it's over with someone who one way or the other is collecting a fee on the way out the door.

I mean, yes, I get it. Ya got laid. Believe me, I get it.

I just wonder if it really accomplishes anything that can't be accomplished . . . shall we say . . . prostitute free. Presumably it's much better, but if it was just a one-time thing I don't know if the frustration level over not having sex would really change. Is it like having one M&M? I don't mean to trivialize the subject—I'm just trying to add a little levity. But I really wonder if having one experience only leads to wanting another even more.

The thought of paying a prostitute on a regular basis seems pathetic to me. I'm at a point in my life where I'm questioning my daily routine. For a few years I've blogged about sports very regularly, sometimes daily, and, like every writer in the world who never gets anywhere, pussyfooted around with a novel. Suddenly, or not so suddenly, I'm wondering where the value is in what I'm doing. I'm certainly not making a living with my writing. Am I really accomplishing anything? I wonder if I'm keeping myself busy with nonsense just to avoid the reality of major boredom in my life. And to some degree I'm trying to make changes.

The point is that I can't imagine transferring what I've been doing in other aspects of my life—potentially fooling myself with hollow activities to feel like I'm doing something—to the sexual part of my life. The theory seems to be, "I'm having sex, so the void is filled."

Well, no, I'd be having sex with a prostitute. Beyond the basics, it wouldn't answer any of the doubts that surround the problem. Will I find love? Will I always be alone?

Able-bodied friends are often quick to point out that these aren't questions strictly for people with disabilities. I'm never quite sure what the point of that is. OK, other people go through it too. And?

Besides, it's different when you have a disability. It is very different.

I can't count the number of times someone has told my mom that she's too young not to have someone in her life. Those same people would never say that to me. Some of her friends politely say how handsome I am. My mom and I have an ongoing joke that only safe woman say such things—her friends who are married and/or old enough to feel secure that I would not be interested in them.

I briefly became friendly with a friend of a friend of my mother who was much closer to my age than my mother's age. The relationship grew very slowly, and I can honestly say there was never that moment when I thought I was in love. It was more like realizing that maybe there could actually be something between us. Going to a movie together came up quite naturally—my mom wasn't interested in the film. Months later, when I got my last job, I invited her and my mom to a celebratory dinner. It seemed to go well. Afterward, my mom had some errands to run, and the friend and I went back to the house.

I thought we had a great talk. Really connected.

And I never saw her again.

Was that date number three? Not really, but I think we both realized that a date would have been the next step. Instead, several casual dinner invitations from me to her were shot down. When one finally came from her it was to my mother for the three of us. I bailed. I can't say for sure she picked up on my potential romantic interest, but for the first time in such matters I protected myself. Either way, she was not interested in me beyond friendship, and I wasn't going to hang on as her friend's disabled son who was a nice guy. To be fair, she never really indicated that I was anything more to her.

So, my frustration and loneliness continued. I deal with it as best I can, and every time a woman sparks my interest, I know I haven't given up on finding someone to love. There are days I wish I *could* give up.

I've heard of at least two people with cerebral palsy much more severe than mine who are married. One is married to a perfectly able-bodied guy. For more brutal and seemingly cold or possibly bitter honesty, when I think about these people I have a hard time believing they're married.

It makes me wonder about all of the selfish and, perhaps, rude questions that seem to come back to one: Why not me?

I guess after 40 years the only thing I actually know of love is that we can definitely miss what we've never had.

June 10, 2012
Regrets from the Easy Road
(previously unpublished)

A person born on the day I graduated high school can legally have a beer as of today. It's a rather strange thought, but maybe it means I'm old enough to pass on another thought that may come frighteningly close to advice.

Occasionally, I joke that I majored in English literature because I was terrible at math. Actually, I was pretty good at math until about the middle of Algebra I in freshman year of high school. That may not sound like much to lament, but the precipitous drop-off of my math skills and the reasons for the decline are something I've been thinking about lately.

When I was being prepared to attend "regular" school, one of the things that was drummed into my head was that my handwriting would be unacceptable in the "real world." It was just part of the program that taught my classmates and me that our special education teachers were the only ones who would have any tolerance whatsoever for our disabilities and that we better be prepared for the evil robots who taught in the mainstream.

Granted, my handwriting wouldn't have received any gold stars from the nuns my older brothers had to deal with. It wasn't terrific for the public school system that was eventually forced to let kids with disabilities attend their schools, either.

But it was good enough for me to learn Pre-Algebra the year before I was mainstreamed. Grades weren't very reliable indicators of the quality of a student's work at the school for kids with disabilities that I attended, but

I'm confident I truly grasped the subject well. Ironically, the "no writing rule" wasn't enforced that year after I rebelled against it. For a while I had tried to obey the rule while using something called a memo-writer. I was supposed to type most of my schoolwork on a machine that printed a maximum of three lines at a time, with no more than 16 characters per line, on a receipt-like strip of paper.

For subjects other than math, the no writing rule didn't really matter. At "special" school, we weren't exactly required to write many long answers and typewriters were readily available on the rare occasions that there was a need to write something beyond a paragraph.

But it was borderline absurd to attempt to do any type of algebraic math on the memo-writer. The machine wasn't suitable for writing out answers to long division problems, let alone more complex equations. I knew it. I said it. I eventually said it loudly, as I tend to do. And I stuck to my conviction . . . until I was mainstreamed beginning in eighth grade.

As far as I was told, this was the real world. No more playing games. Those evil regular ed teachers would just fail me if they couldn't read what I wrote. Years before I was mainstreamed I even heard the words, "No teacher is going to sit with you and try to figure out what you wrote." I was so nervous by the time I attended my first day of regular school that out of nowhere I developed the habit of holding my neck with my right hand to try to stabilize myself. I was waiting for laser beams to shoot out of my teachers' eyes and disintegrate me.

Eventually, of course, I settled in. My teachers turned out to be normal human beings. They were even nice. But I wasn't about to question the "no writing rule."

For a year, not using my handwriting wasn't a problem for a very simple reason—I was doing Pre-Algebra again with the exact same textbook. I wasn't attempting to learn something new by seeing it one way on a blackboard and typing it another way on a machine that was in no way made to do math.

I began to struggle with math by the middle of freshman year in high school. Gone were the nice middle school teachers, including supportive resource room staff who were there to smooth over problems students with disabilities might be having in the mainstream. They were replaced with an Algebra I teacher who I still think actually would have shot laser beams at me if he had been capable of it—the man was not pleased about having to move to a different room every seventh period due to the lack of an elevator in the school at the time—and a resource room teacher and aide who were focused on completing their own degrees and simply didn't feel like doing their jobs most days.

The memo-writer was also essentially gone shortly after high school began, as supplies for the machine were no longer available. I began working exclusively on an early laptop that I had received the summer before eighth grade to use in conjunction with the memo-writer. The screen displayed seven lines of text less than half the length of a line of paper. It was an improvement, but the Zygo was still essentially a typewriter without the ability to print in class—which just thrilled already skeptical teachers.

It wasn't long before I couldn't even see half of the solution to the math problem that I was working on. The first lines of my answer scrolled up too far, and each line of the solution would "word wrap" to a second line on the word processor. Typed solutions to Algebra equations simply didn't look right. Just as importantly, typing a solution took longer than writing the answers by hand (even for me) and just had a different feel than writing the problem down with a pencil and paper.

By January I was frustrated and barely getting by with Cs. I had made the honor roll every quarter the year before. Geometry followed sophomore year, and the subject brought more struggles. Then came Algebra II, followed by Trigonometry and Advanced Math. Let's just say that when my Trig teacher asked me what I was majoring in at college, his face lit up like a Christmas tree when I said English literature.

Believe it or not, my point isn't that I got screwed by everyone else. There were some honest mistakes and a bad teacher or two along the way. But the biggest mistake made was all mine.

I didn't take control of the situation.

On some level I knew what was going on. I got genuinely frustrated, and I honestly can't understand why I never trusted my instincts and picked up a damn pencil. By the time I knew I was in real trouble as far as learning Algebra I, I feared being held back.

I also knew I could take the easy road: I could pass the course without truly learning the material. The fact of the matter was that I wasn't going to fail as long as I showed some effort.

I failed my first social studies test in high school. I failed it because I hadn't studied hard enough. It was the first class I ever had in which students took note after note on lectures during every class and were eventually tested on the material. Studying the night before didn't cut it. I failed because I was completely unprepared—and no other reason.

A few days after the original test I easily passed the makeup exam. The resource room teacher told me that the social studies teacher said I was just nervous and did better with the "other type of test." The other type of test was the B-level test, which I was surprised to receive when my class took our second test of the semester. I remember looking into the eyes of some of my A-level classmates when they saw the teacher give me the easier test. It was embarrassing. But for some reason, I accepted it.

I was given the easy way out and I took it. I did very well on the second test, again, because I had studied hard. Once I understood that I would be receiving the easier test on a regular basis, my resolve to do better diminished. I went back to barely studying and pulled about a C in the class.

Teachers weren't necessarily being nice in these types of situations. They were also taking the easy way out. With a few wonderful exceptions, regular ed teachers didn't want to deal too much with the disabled students. As my ninth grade science teacher once told me when I was struggling, "If your mom comes in here, we're going to have a problem." He didn't want the hassle—and he was actually a good guy. He was much happier to tell me not to worry and let me slide. (He also didn't know Mom was genuinely old school, and I mean that as a compliment. She wouldn't have gone to school to blame a teacher if I wasn't doing well in a particular class. I have a great mom, and her first question when there was a problem with any of her sons at school asked what we did wrong.)

The next year I dropped down to B-level social studies without even being told to do so. B-level was where enthusiasm for a subject went to die. Teachers were convinced students were stupid—disabled or not—on the first day of school and didn't push them at all.

Math was a different story. Every year I started with a renewed resolve to do better. In fact, I always started strong. Then the solutions to problems got longer, frustration settled in, I would barely do my homework—and I got away with it.

I look back and I know I have all the excuses I could ever want for not doing what I needed to do. I was a kid. I was the disabled kid in the big, bad mainstream of regular school. The resource room staff was useless my first two years and in a state of flux my last two. Teachers were letting me slide by doing just enough.

Whether or not doing better in high school math or some other classes would have changed anything in my life is something I'll never know. To be clear, I did OK in other classes, but I always knew when I could slide and when I couldn't play games. Science was always tough for me, partly because I had almost no experience with it before being mainstreamed, but a department-wide use of multiple-choice tests and some sliding got me through. I took a computer course for three years that made future college courses a breeze, but I did well in it thanks in part to a teacher who refused to accept anything except my best.

English was my best subject by far and I always wanted to be a writer anyway. So pursuing a degree in English literature wasn't exactly a burden. It's possible I would have followed that path even if I had maintained my math skills.

I got my act together at college. As I killed time between classes on my second day as a commuter student, I realized that no one was going to make me go to my next class, let alone let me get away with half-assed efforts. Professors didn't care if I failed. They barely knew my name, and I was the only student with a disability (at least an obvious physical one) in all but one or two of my classes. Failing me wasn't going to lead to what high school teachers feared would be a big to-do with parents, an upset disabled student, and God knew what else in their minds. There was no more sliding by.

I finally took control. It was far from easy, and the university was anything but welcoming to students with disabilities at the time. But I worked hard and graduated with honors.

Had I taken control sooner, maybe I would have taken a few accounting classes along the way instead of just surviving the one math course that was required. Maybe a few more doors would be open if I had become a better student in high school.

At the very least, I would know that I had done my best. I believe knowing that I didn't do my best is the reason I still think about the erosion of my math skills from time to time.

The reason I chose to write about the deterioration of those skills isn't to whine or wallow. I don't know if I'll ever have the relationship with my nieces and nephews that would allow me to pass on the message of pushing themselves when no one is doing it for them. But as I've written in the past, I think it's especially important for the disability community to share such lessons.

Those of us with disabilities may always find it harder than our able-bodied counterparts to follow through on what we know to be best for ourselves. We're not taught to do so when others are given such lessons. We're often taught that we are to be taken care of—a well-intentioned message that can steal our instincts to be strong and care for ourselves.

There are often physical reasons that might make others who are seemingly in control discourage us from following our instincts. Typing was physically easier than writing for me (and the result was easier for others to read), but it wasn't always the best way for me to learn. In high school, I often borrowed notes from other kids because it was easier. In college, I had to take my own notes and I learned that the act of taking the notes helped me retain the information better. Learning to study didn't hurt either.

I'm still learning these lessons. I'm not very good at pushing myself beyond my comfort zone. Allowing others to lead the way is often easier for everyone, and it's generally expected of people with disabilities. Yet, those other people won't be the ones living with the results.

People with disabilities have enough obstacles to deal with. We don't need to put more in our own way by taking the easy road.

Wednesday, December 23, 2009
Three Decades Later, A Christmas Memory of
    Working for Independence

I rolled my eyes when Val pulled the bus over to talk to the guy in the wheelchair who she waved to every day on the way home. A general groan went up as we realized she was taking time to buy some of the Christmas cards he tried to sell on the sidewalk of a string of stores somewhere near Springfield.

We just wanted to get home from school, which for some of us wasn't until well after 4 p.m. on days that started around 6 a.m. Door-to-door bus service for kids with disabilities who lived throughout the county and attended a centralized "special" school came with prices some never realized. I'll confess that 7:30 a.m. to 4 p.m. was the worst I ever had it.

If I remember correctly, the cards the guy in the wheelchair was selling were homemade, which back then meant he might have been able to run off copies of an original on a Xerox machine. This was even before the days of Print Shop, so he had probably drawn the original scenes by hand.

I no doubt wondered, if I even cared to think about it, why the guy wasn't doing something more with his life. Now, nearly 30 years later I admire the guy whose name I don't remember. He was, in fact, trying to do something with his life.

Coming to the end of year number five with The Stores @ Royal Steele, I can't help but think about that guy. I've driven past the spot where he used to be many times (again, if memory serves), and don't ever recall seeing him after that school year. In the arrogance of youth, I would see older guys with disabilities and swear I'd never be like them. It occurs to me that—from the little I knew of him, anyway—I'm not all that different from the guy who sold Christmas cards to Val.

Just recently I was sure I would surpass the $500 mark in all-time profits from my website, which I had planned to invest in a certificate of deposit. I didn't expect much, but thought I'd have a shot at covering the cost of the website for a year with the interest. Instead I learned that my bank requires 10 times the amount I've earned to open a CD, and the interest on that amount would barely cover about a year and a half of the website's cost.

It was a reminder of how little I know about the business world, and how very far I am from turning the website into a worthwhile business. Yet, I will give it another year. I suspect my reasons are similar to those of the guy who kept going out in the December cold to sell his cards.

As I've said before, it's my effort to do something productive in my life, to do something besides live off Social Security.

I've worked full-time for a leading publisher of children's books. I have experience writing for the **Philadelphia Inquirer.** I recently completed a two-year stint on a grant at a foundation which claimed its mission was to enhance the lives of people with disabilities. Yet, these experiences have solidified my belief that the only way I will ever find success in the professional sense will be through independent efforts. The message, even from organizations most assume would be anxious to find qualified employees with disabilities, has been clear. Some were willing to "let" me work to keep busy, while another was glad to have me as a poster child, but giving me an opportunity to build a career with them was never truly part of their plan.

Looking beyond my experience as an employee, my time in the so-called advocacy world re-focused my attention on an elemental problem facing people with disabilities. All too often the very core of what this and many other government-funded programs do to "advocate" for people with disabilities is to hand out grants.

Of course, in most cases, an individual must be dirt poor to receive a grant. In fact, I have been counseled by so-called advocates, including my former boss, on the value of hiding assets in order to qualify for grant money.

Many people with disabilities are never even taught to try to be financially self-sufficient. It is the most self-defeating message imaginable, and keeps the so-called advocates in business by ensuring that people with disabilities need their grants.

People with significant physical disabilities who are mentally and physically capable of leading independent lives need a new message. We need to take control of our own financial futures and stop celebrating the idea of grants that require us to be broke.

I am not suggesting that we turn down money available to us. With the realities of finding employment and health care concerns, that would be absurd. I certainly don't do it. I also know that it will take much more than a "just do it" mentality to take control of our financial futures. However, rejecting the message that we should seek "funding" as opposed to attempting to generate income to support a lifestyle we want can be a start.

As a new year and a new decade begins, my goal will continue to be to build Royal Steele into something worthwhile. When I first started my website, part of the "About Us" was my "ultimate goal" of helping to build a recreation center geared toward people with disabilities. I removed it when I connected the site to a charity, but the concept has never left my thoughts.

In the new year I plan to reinstate the idea of building a rec center as part of "About Us." My goal may never be reached, but I think that at least having such a goal may be a step in the right direction. Attempts to donate to established charities as a step toward doing something positive for the disability community have convinced me even more that people with disabilities must work toward taking control of our own advocacy and financial well-being.

Once this year's commissions are paid, I will make a donation directly to a sports club for wheelchair users. In three years I will have donated more than 15% of all-time profits generated by commissions from a project that has made slightly more than $600 (including advertising revenue) and was in the red until August of 2008. In fact, the first donation in 2007 was made strictly from profits in November and December because the website was in the red for the other 10 months. But I found a way to make a donation from money generated by the website that year to demonstrate that I was serious about doing something positive.

Yet, efforts to truly work with an advocacy group in what I hoped would be a mutually beneficial situation have been unsuccessful. In an e-mail I wasn't supposed to see, a staff member of one non-profit suggested not working with me because I couldn't donate enough money. In previous years, contractual agreements to promote my efforts to donate to another non-profit (for which I briefly worked) as part of their fundraising were essentially ignored. To my knowledge, both organizations are run by, and the second is now 100 percent staffed by, able-bodied people.

As angry and disappointed as such dealings make me, they also make me push harder to turn my own efforts into something worthwhile. I recently launched PhillyACCESS, a user-driven source of information and opinions from the disability community of Philadelphia and surrounding areas. I will also continue to write about these issues and encourage others to join the discussion. Most of all, I will keep working to make The Stores @ Royal Steele a viable business.

Right now, my efforts probably aren't much more than the 2000s equivalent of hoofing it out to the sidewalk to sell Christmas cards made by hand. In fact, the guy I remember from that long-ago December probably had a lot more guts doing what he did than I do trying to make the website a financially worthwhile business.

But I'd like to think our efforts have at least one thing in common: the hope of building something that would contribute, in however small a way, toward making the disability community an economically viable one for people with disabilities instead of those working as advocates. That's not meant as a condemnation of all advocacy groups for people with disabilities run by the able-bodied. Instead, it's a restating of what some have said long before me. People with disabilities must make more efforts to become financially independent as individuals and as a group. All other forms of independence hinge on it.

Monday, May 31, 2010
Training for the M.S. Ride Bringing More than
   Expected

All winter I watched the electronic display on the exercise bike, wondering if it was really going to translate to the road. I could go longer and further than ever before, the number of miles and minutes finally reaching levels that seemed significant without the polite angle of "considering the disability . . ." But was it real?

The mere fact that I can use the words "translate to the road" is amazing to me. From the first time I reluctantly tried a hand-cycle, I've been addicted to biking.

My mom and I had driven to an adaptive cycling program on a Saturday morning. I had been told the program had a foot-pedaled trike, which was the type of cycle I was looking to try. I was disappointed to learn that the program didn't actually own the type of cycle I wanted to try, but since we were already there I took the opportunity to use a hand-cycle.

That first day I went about three miles. Transitioning to the foot-pedaled trike of a volunteer at the program a month or so later, I did about five miles. At the time I was hovering around 10 miles on the exercise bike. But it wasn't about the miles. Not yet, anyway.

I was 36 years old, and it was the first time I'd been on a bike since I was about 10. Far from a nature lover, I knew instantly that passing trees as opposed to watching a readout was the way to go. Being outdoors with the smell of the grass, and the dirt, and even the Schuylkill River, made it all feel a bit more real.

As time went by, my competitive side kicked into gear. For better or worse, I started noticing that I was one of the slowest riders in the program. The first time I heard about people from the program doing the M.S. Ride, I had only cycled about five times and didn't even own a bike yet. But the seed was planted. The thought of working toward such a specific physical goal—one that seemed rather daunting though not completely impossible—appealed to me as though I'd unknowingly been waiting for it to come along.

By the following summer I began thinking about actually attempting the M.S. Ride, but I knew I wasn't ready. The volunteers at the program suggested doing part of the first day (it's a two-day event), but simply participating wasn't what appealed to me about doing the ride. If I was going to do it, I was going to really do it.

Time after time in my life I have worked at physical activities, thinking I was truly accomplishing something, only to learn it had been a "nice" thing considering my disability. That's not a cry for pity; I've done OK in other ways, thank you. But in the sports arena I love so much, I've never really accomplished anything tangible.

Just a couple years ago my doctor told me that my "good" cholesterol was low and wondered aloud if exercise was out of the question. I'd been working out four or five days a week. In high school I actually attempted to join the wrestling team. One day while I was "running," which for me meant pushing very slowly through the halls in my manual chair, another wrestler came up from behind and started pushing me. He said something about it helping him coast, and besides, I wasn't moving fast enough to get in shape anyway. Before being mainstreamed I played wheelchair hockey in school for years, improving as I grew, but knowing we were "playing amongst ourselves" and that competing with able-bodied kids wasn't likely. (Years later, I figured out that was OK, but as a kid it was always on my mind.) I've lifted weights or used the Total Gym for years, and while I've seen mild improvements, I never really approached the strength of my able-bodied brothers, who are pretty much typical weekend warriors.

Three months from now, I'll be attempting the M.S. Ride. When I hear the biking-program volunteers with whom I'll be riding tell me about all the safeguards along the 75-mile route, I know they just want to build my confidence. But there's a part of me that doesn't want to hear about the safeguards.

There is something unmistakably "real" about biking for me. At the end of the season last October, I finally got up the nerve to try the eight-mile loop that others were doing. Beginning at the program's boathouse on the western bank of the Schuylkill River, the route follows Martin Luther King Jr. Drive north to Falls Bridge. After crossing the river, the loop follows Kelly Drive all the way to the Philadelphia Museum of Art. Bending around the museum, the route turns back toward the boathouse. By the time I seriously considered attempting the loop, the distance (which I've since learned is actually about 8.6 miles) was only part of my concern.

Most of the cyclists who rode with volunteers tended to stay on MLK Drive, and while I was already riding on my own, I always knew a volunteer wasn't far off. Crossing Falls Bridge pretty much felt like going over the horizon leaving Spain with Columbus. The "what ifs" were getting to me, mostly the one that said, "What if I got a flat?" Sure, I had a cell phone with me, and I eventually would have been able to explain what happened to people who were just starting to get to know me and understand my speech. But even people who really know me struggle to understand my speech on the cell sometimes, and I'd never actually seen anyone answer a phone at the boathouse or even seen the phone, and, well, what if . . . ?

But with the cycle program closing for the season in a few weeks, I knew my chances to try the loop were dwindling, not to come again for months. A bigger "what if" arose in my head: What if I wimp out and let the obstacle grow in my head for another five months when biking started up again in April? So, as I got to the Falls Bridge, the place I usually turned around, I made a right turn and crossed the bridge to Kelly Drive.

Eight-plus miles later, I made it back to the boathouse just fine.

But I was beat. The thought of doing almost 10 times the distance seemed like a far cry from a good idea.

Quite frankly, it doesn't exactly seem like the stuff of genius as I write on Memorial Day weekend, six months later. But as I stared at the digital display all winter, I never stopped thinking about it.

Seventy-five miles.

I hit the ground running in April, doing the loop week one. So far I've done as many as three consecutive laps on a few Saturdays this season, with only an abundance of foot traffic keeping me from a fourth once or twice. My Memorial Day weekend included a Saturday ride of 25+ miles in three 8.6-mile segments done in 48, 43, and 50 minutes. My total time, including breaks, was 2 1/2 hours.

Preparing for the M.S. Ride has been incredibly motivating. It's a real thing that won't be accomplished by anything short of getting on my bike and pedaling 75 miles, with a lot more training mixed in between now and then. But something else has happened in the last couple of weeks.

Knowing that the weekly cycling program was going to be cancelled a few times in upcoming weeks because of other events being held by the river on Saturdays, and that the exercise bike was good but not a substitute for the real thing, I very recently bit the bullet and headed down to MLK Drive on my own during the week. I had been thinking about it for a while, and I knew it was time to start pushing through some of my fears. Easier said than done, especially with a disability, but I finally did it.

A couple days prior to my first solo ride in Philly, it hit me that I used to drive Route 202—a highway known locally for its tight on-ramps and often severe congestion—with no problem when my brother lived in King of Prussia. Now, I avoid Route 202 like the plague. In not driving the highway regularly, I lost my nerve to deal with that level of traffic.

It was time to start getting some of that type of nerve back. Time to stop listening to the "what ifs."

So, of course, the first thing that happened on my inaugural solo trip to the Schuylkill River as I rode my bike out of my wheelchair-accessible (and now bike-accessible) van was that I knocked the bike chain off. In the past, I'd always needed help fixing it. But, I had no choice, and I fixed it. Even if I had wanted to cut bait and go home, I couldn't. I can only get my bike in the car by pedaling up the ramp. Having no safety net can help sometimes, I guess!

The actual ride went smoothly. In some ways it was nicer than Saturday rides because there were very few people out. I only did one loop though, as the only accessible port-a-potty I knew of was locked. But it was a start.

Able to relax on successive solo trips, I've gotten more out of each ride. I located other accessible port-a-potties that are open all week (no small concern). I have increased my ride to two loops, confident I have the strength to do the extra miles and still be able to handle things that go along with taking the actual ride—like getting back in the car. This is harder than it sounds after a fatiguing ride, especially when I have to deal with more spasticity than I usually do because I'm still a little nervous about riding on my own in the city. I have even begun focusing on improving my speed on the trike. (I don't want to be the guy they're waiting on at the finish line before they can pack up!)

The "what ifs" still require a deep breath to get past each time I decide to head down to Philly solo. But at the moment, they aren't winning the battle.

I'm not a "rah, rah, everything is awesome" type of guy. I was taught to be realistic, to know my limits. I don't believe in people with disabilities having phony "I can do anything" attitudes. I tend to focus on what I can do independently, and try to build on those things. But the friends I'm making through adaptive cycling are teaching me that there's a middle ground.

I've become one of the stronger riders of the group after the winter of workouts. I would be lying if I said that didn't feel good. Having this tangible goal has already been a tremendous experience, helping me become physically stronger. Yet, the unexpected baby steps to becoming mentally stronger have been just as valuable.

My friends joke that I'm a "monster" after I do a long ride on a Saturday. Yet, one of them is a lawyer who travels independently whenever he wants, without fear of his disability getting in his way. Another has a high-level role in a different adaptive sports program. Still another has a family and a long-term career, battling past the prejudice he never mentions but no doubt faced. The list goes on.

In September, I have every intention of pedaling my way across the entire 75-mile course of the M.S. Ride. I'll remember my friends from school, and celebrate the effort with some new friends. Regardless of the ultimate outcome, though, I believe the challenge has already made me stronger in ways I never anticipated. I can only hope it has started me on a path that translates into being as strong as the real "monsters" of strength I'm getting to know better every Saturday.

Thursday, September 30, 2010
M.S. Ride 2010 with Team PCAS

Ten feet from the top of the second causeway heading into Ocean City, I was scared to death that I was going to come up just that short of my goal of completing the 75-mile course of the 2010 M.S. City to Shore Bike Ride on a solo trike. I could see Reid Overturf, who had graciously sacrificed his ride to stay with me all day, looking back giving me a thumbs-up. John Siemiarowski, another volunteer from the Pennsylvania Center for Adapted Sports, along with his tandem partner, Bruce Linsky, were behind me offering the brand of sarcastic support only guys seem to get. And all I could think of was that my lunch was suddenly ready to make a rare encore appearance and that John was going to turn out to be prophetic.

John had consistently told me as I prepared for the ride that I could tandem with him to the finish line if necessary. Later, he said that he would just get me over the causeways if I needed it, and he seemed certain I would. He and Bruce, having reached Ocean City, had biked back to go with me as I went over the causeways, "just in case."

Looking back, it was appropriate that both Reid and John were there as I attempted to cross the causeways. Reid went with me on my first bike ride with PCAS, which was about three miles on a hand-cycle. And I never really get into biking without John's generosity in sharing his foot-pedaled trike at the very beginning as I decided whether or not buying my own made sense. It's something he does with every newcomer, and it's a great example to see throughout the summer.

The day had actually started at 12:40 in the morning for me. That was the time when I checked the clock after I was forced to admit that my plan to go to bed a little earlier every night and wake up earlier every morning that week had failed miserably. The idea was to be able to wake up at 4 a.m. ready to ride 75 miles on Saturday. Nerves had gotten the best of me and, I feared, ended my hopes of completing the ride. A not-so-nice chat with God and my old man somehow worked, and the next thing I knew I was waking up a minute before my mom came downstairs and turned the light on to wake me.

Amazingly, my early morning angst would be the only thing to go wrong for me all day.

Team PCAS started with several guys with visual disabilities and another with multiple sclerosis each on a tandem with a volunteer, and myself on a pedal trike being followed closely by Reid. There was also, I believe, at least one solo volunteer rider.

Early on, it paid off to have participated in Bike Philly just a couple weeks prior. I was prepared for starting an event with a lot of bikes. Certainly, the M.S. Ride had hundreds, if not thousands more, but I had a feel for riding in a group. Quite frankly, I also had a feel for dealing with the basic human needs, which was a lifesaver. Let's just say that exhaustion, cerebral palsy, and port-a-potties wasn't a mixture I was going to test when a jar in the back of the support vehicle would suffice.

By coincidence, Bike Philly was on my dad's birthday, so I wore the purple band on my arm from the Alzheimer's Walk that our family had done years ago. Dad's been gone since 1997. I wore the band again on Saturday.

My mom was with me every bit of the day, too. That "support vehicle" was actually my van, driven rest stop to rest stop by my mom all day long in amazing support of my effort. Without my mom, Reid, John, and everybody at PCAS, I simply don't even attempt the M.S. Ride.

But I had, in fact, decided to attempt it, and the incredible response I received from just one e-mail seeking donations to meet my requirement to the M.S. Society made it clear that there was no bailing out. As the day approached, the seemingly constant e-mailed reminders from the volunteers (who just wanted everything to go well) to each member of the group about supplies, last-minute preparations, and various other details, made it hard to try to not think "too much" about the ride. I had prepared as much as possible, and I just wanted to get to it.

A sports fan my whole life, I never played Little League, CYO, or pee-wee football. I never fit into the few programs that were available to kids with disabilities 30 years ago, and don't fit many adult programs now. I'm either too able or not able enough. Discovering biking with PCAS three summers ago has been the best thing I've ever found, and Saturday felt like my first official "game."

Finally, we were pulling out of the starting area—it wasn't really a line—sometime before 7 a.m. Adrenaline was taking care of the sleep issues. Our teammates were quickly out of sight—though not quite as long as they thought they'd be. From the start, Reid was simply awesome, offering little pieces of advice but still letting us just ride and enjoy. Eventually, his ability to keep me focused was huge. About nine hours on a bike can cause the mind to wander, which can bring an unexpected end to the day. I was brought back from drifting a few times.

Luck was with us all day, including at the very beginning. As we got started, a woman I knew only as

"Mary"—I kid you not—said hello and "God bless you." The words literally weren't out of her mouth when she was slammed from behind and the pile-up was on. I'm thinking God prefers to offer his own blessings. Fortunately, we didn't get caught in it, and, quite frankly, our good fortune never ended. We didn't have a single technical problem, flat tire, or any other problem all day.

While I feared hearing "on your left" in my head until Christmas, the refrain bikers use when passing wasn't all I heard. A lot of people said things like, "Way to go" and "Keep going" as they passed. Some merely offered a thumbs-up, and it was actually very nice. Not long ago that type of attention might have rankled me, as I would have felt like I was being patronized. But I think the other cyclists were just offering a genuine show of respect for being part of a difficult ride. In fact, Reid put a funny twist on it, frequently wondering aloud, "What about me?"

One woman in particular stood out. She recovered nicely after asking Reid if I had cerebral palsy and I gave the affirmative answer. She got the message and started speaking directly to me. Asking what my number was, she teased me for not remembering it. Talking takes some effort for me, and I had zero energy to waste, so I refrained from pointing out that it was on the back of my bike and that she was coming up from behind. I merely sped up to show her my rider number—4469. She said something about wanting to let the M.S. Society know I had participated.

Reid would later mention that he hoped I would remember all the people that wanted to say hello or touch base in some way that day. And I will. But I think he knew that the memory, while it wouldn't be a bad one, would be remembered through the light of the end result. I had a goal, and we were still a long way from achieving it.

The first inkling I had that we were doing OK, beyond just a mindset that I was going to finish—which sounds good but doesn't move a bike very far—came after the second rest stop. I felt surprisingly good, and I started to realize we were keeping up a decent pace. I heard a couple people say, "There's that cool bike again."

Again? I realized that they must have passed me before, and somehow we had passed them in turn.

We had actually caught up to our teammates at that rest stop, I believe. They do tend to run together. John joked that they were clearly at the rest stop too long if we had reached them. It was the only rest stop we were able to pretty much blow in and out of.

In fact, at the 30-mile mark, we were actually leading the entire team. I know—it wasn't a race. But considering that everyone else who participated as a member of PCAS was doing a tandem, and the one other guy with a physical disability was doing only part of the ride, I was feeling good. I felt even better when I was serenaded with "The Mighty Quinn" as the other PCAS riders soon passed by for the final time until the end. They tease me about being a sports fan and a bit competitive, but I now know for sure that I'm not the only one with a competitive streak.

At 40 miles, I was in unchartered waters, having never done a longer training ride. Soon—or more accurately, eventually—miles 50 and 60 passed. Time meshes together, but at one point boats on the bay seemed pretty damned inviting as we passed. Pain in my thighs from earlier hadn't lasted for some reason. Nor did the strain in my inner right thigh, which usually signals the beginning of the end of a day of training for me.

Feeling good was over by the last rest stop. There was no specific pain, but fatigue was setting in. It was time to gut it out. There was less than 20 miles left. It was less than two loops at the Schuylkill River, if the path behind the Art Museum is counted, where PCAS meets every Saturday. The distance was nothing.

But those miles included the causeways into Ocean City.

I hadn't heard much about the causeways, or I had simply blocked the information out, until the last couple weeks. Luckily, I couldn't even picture them in my head, as I'm quite sure my Friday night panic attack would have been much worse. The warnings from Reid started to hit home in a Monday night planning session. By then I was overloaded with information and couldn't really process much.

The concerns were well intentioned, but I had tired a bit of the suggestions that I get in the car for the causeways or tandem over them. It was part of ride, the challenge, and my goal was to finish the ride—not some of it or even most of it. All of it.

My dad used to say, "It's not how strong you are, it's how long you're strong." I was going to find out whether I was strong enough to finish the 75-mile version of the M.S. Ride.

That said, it started to occur to me that Reid and John were the strongest riders I knew, and that if they were so focused on the causeways, there was likely reason for concern.

My mom offered to wait by the bridges in case I couldn't do it. After a moment of thought, I asked her to just go to the finish line. I didn't want to have any "outs."

We were about 45 minutes behind our team as we approached the bridges. I know this because Reid got a call on his cell from John. I saw Reid using his phone a few times that day, mostly reading or responding to texts, and I later joked that he was catching up on his correspondences as he followed me throughout the day. The tandem riders were deciding whether or not to wait for us. John and Bruce were headed back for moral support.

Connecting with John and Bruce after hitting some heavy traffic, I was told we'd arrived too fast because the guy driving John's truck had been caught in traffic too. I didn't even realize what he had meant until later. John didn't have the bike that could tandem with mine.

Finally, Reid told me that we were about to turn a corner and see the causeways.

The final scene of *Planet of the Apes*—in which Charlton Heston sees the Statue of Liberty—comes to mind in describing what I saw. I can't say that I actually thought anything when I first got a look at the concrete monstrosities sticking out of the water. I just had an incredibly sharp, quick feeling of what I can only assume was fear. I can only assume that, because as fast as the feeling came it was gone. I have heard that your mind only allows you to deal with what you can deal with, and that's the only explanation I have for what happened.

Pedal. Just pedal. Pedal your damn bike.

That's all I could think. As we approached the first bridge, Reid and I executed a plan where he helped me shift the main gear into the easiest gear for the bike. My left arm is very spastic, and I struggle to work that gear when I am just starting a leisurely ride. By then, I was barely able to get my right gear down to 3. I couldn't get lower.

Forget it. Just pedal. Keep moving the bike.

Over the first concrete monstrosity, the guys seemed to take a little joy in warning me that the "big one" was next.

I remember seeing what seemed like a lot of people on the side of the bridge. I think at least one was walking.

All I truly remember is knowing that I just needed to keep pedaling.

Keep moving your legs. I don't care how slow you move, just don't stop.

I saw Reid look back, smiling. I could see the bridge crest like a wave reaching its peak and disappear as it sloped downward on the other side. John, an incredibly strong rider, was talking the whole time.

Pedal. Pedal. I suddenly felt like I was going to barf. I wondered if I should keep pedaling if I did.

Shut up and just f—ing pedal!

I did it.

We did it.

We were heading down the second causeway. We might as well have had wings.

It was all over but a nice, easy ride through Ocean City—my dad's favorite place to vacation.

The rest of the team waited for us, an amazing gesture on their part. We stopped to take pictures, which turned out to be a blessing. My mom later informed me that she was stuck in traffic, and a friend of the family who had also done the ride helped her negotiate her way to the finish in time to see us.

As the picture taking ended, John said something like, "Ok, we gotta get going. We're holding up Rob!" It was hilarious. I learned that when they made the ride back to Philadelphia on Sunday, they did a toast at the finish, and it included "to Rob Quinn." It was overwhelming to hear about.

I lost track of Reid for a few minutes, then realized he was ahead of me. I sped up, thinking that we just had to finish together after a nine-hour day. What I didn't realize was that Team PCAS had all come together, and allowed me to cross the line first.

Seventy-five miles—done!

I'm told it was actually about 77 miles, and I pedaled solo through every inch of the course! It was easily the best physical accomplishment of my life, and a day I'll never forget. Without my mom, Reid, John, and everyone at Team PCAS, it simply does not happen. As a writer, it's not easy to say that words can't express my appreciation, but they really cannot. All I can do is say THANK YOU to them for everything.

About the Author

Rob J. Quinn started as a freelance writer for the *Philadelphia Inquirer* Sports section, and wrote a series of articles on the disability community for the local section of the paper. He moved on to eventually work full-time as an editor with a children's book publisher, and wrote a book for the publisher on a freelance basis. Quinn then spent several years blogging. His sports blog, *Rob Q. Ink,* was often quoted in the *Inquirer's* "Blog Zone" section of the paper. On *Rob Q. Ink—Page 2,* the writer offered thoughts on various topics, including the disability community.

Learn more about the author and *I'm Not Here to Inspire You* at http://robjquinn.blogspot.com/. The site also offers links to find him on Facebook and Twitter, as well as other contact information.